TOP TACTICS FOR BIG TENCH

Tony Miles

First Published in 2014

Copyright   Tony Miles

All rights reserved. No part of this publication may be reproduced or transmitted
In any form or by any means, electronic or mechanical, including photocopy,
Recording or any information storage and retrieval system without permission
in writing from the publishers

British Library Cataloguing in Publication Data

Miles, Tony 1944 –

Top Tactics for Big Tench

ISBN: 9781503253070

Dedications

I owe my thanks to the many manufacturers who supply me with superb products to use in my tench fishing. Special thanks must go To Tini and Simon Pomeroy of Pallatrax, Matt Hayes, Alan Crawford-Plane and Colin Thomas of TFG, Chris Hornsby of Enterprise Tackle, Neil Kiddier of Kamasan and Gary Barclay of Drennan and ESP.

Surprisingly, few of my angling friends are as heavily into big tench as I am, and most of my tenching has been a solitary affair. However, one man who does share my passion for tench, especially river tench, is my good friend Alan Lawrence. Over the last two years we have conducted a most enjoyable campaign together on the Ouse.

As with all my books, I once again dedicate this book to Fran, my wife of almost forty nine years. As I have said so often, without her love, encouragement and understanding, I would never have been able to realise my ambitions and achieve the success I have. To this I must now add outstanding courage, for the remarkably brave manner in which she faced and beat lung cancer in 2007. Fran is a special lady indeed.

My good friend Alan Lawrence with a chunky Ouse specimen

CONTENTS

Introduction

Location

Prebaiting

Hookbaits

Methods & Tactics

Tench Water Comparisons

Care & Conservation

Targeting Extra Big Tench

Big Tench Tales

Conclusion

Introduction

Ever since I felt the silky smoothness of a tench as a young child, the species has been a firm favourite. After carp, tench must be the second most popular still water species, with scores of anglers dedicated to their pursuit to the exclusion of all others. There has never been a better chance to catch a huge tench than there is today. When I first began serious specimen hunting in the late fifties, the benchmark for big tench was five pounds. Few anglers had landed one that big and as for six pounders, they were the stuff of dreams. I remember the late great Richard Walker telling me that he had caught very few tench over five pounds and considered four pounds as the specimen weight.

How things have changed. From around the mid seventies, for whatever reason, tench weights began to escalate rapidly. When I first fished TC pit in 1977, six pounders had become common, sevens were not that rare and the benchmark for exceptional fish had now reached eight pounds. At Deans Farm in 1984, where I increased my best to 8lbs 14ozs, the tench world had witnessed the first authenticated double figure fish in the 10lb 1oz fish to Eric Edwards.

If we fast forward to the late nineties, double figure tench were now becoming common. My best ever catch of six fish for 60lbs was taken in 1998, and that included what is still my personal best of 11lb 11ozs. That was then, and still is an exceptional fish and was one of the biggest tench ever taken in Britain. Even in 2004, there had only been about thirty fish caught to beat it. Now, however, eleven and twelve pound fish have become almost commonplace. Indeed, as I write, four twelve pounders and a thirteen pounder have been reported in the last week. Amongst coarse fish, the ultimate growth of tench over the last fifty years has been extraordinary. Most coarse fish species have shown similar gains, but I would submit that none have matched the tench.

The ever expanding availability of gravel pits and large windswept reservoirs has brought specimen tench fishing within the reach of all anglers, for there is no doubt that it these waters that have the greatest potential to produce monsters. However, do not fall into the trap of setting your sights too high or you will risk disillusionment. If you only have access to quiet little estate lakes, ponds, canals or weedy rivers, the chances of a double figure tench are still remote. In fact, some of the most enjoyable tench fishing I do is on the river Ouse. There, as with most rivers, a six pounder is exceptional and sevens are rare. My personal best Ouse tench of 8lb 2oz I rate as highly as my three doubles from a large reservoir.

It only remains to say enjoy your tench fishing and I hope this book helps in some towards achieving that.

Location

1/ Gravel Pits

As with all gravel pit species, tench will be attracted to features such as bars, drop offs, plateaux and so on. I particularly favour the tops of shallow bars and the downward slopes of gentle drop offs. When I think back to all the gravel pit tenching I have done over the years, the most reliable swim type of all has to be the sparsely weeded gravel bar crest amid deeper water which is more heavily weeded. In swims of this type, I feel the tench spend much of their time in the thick vegetation, moving on to the slopes and tops of bars to feed. The bars do not need to be weed free for good tenching, as they usually do for gravel pit bream, and a very successful ploy is to run a weed rake across an intended bar before baiting, if it is too thickly weeded for efficient bait presentation. Again, this is in contrast to bream, for which swim raking has never yielded me any success. Obviously, if you are starting tenching in early spring, you should find such areas sparsely weeded in any event. I have to admit, though, that I rarely rake swims these days. Tench feed happily enough in weed and with modern pop up rigs bait presentation is no problem At Horseshoe Lake I have caught lots of good tench fishing rubber corn or popped up rubber maggots as much as nine inches off the bottom in very thick weed.

Shallow bars and plateaux can easily be seen on clear calm days, but where deeper features need to be located the bankside geography provides useful information. Where it is very gently shelving it usually indicates a similar gentle drop off into the pit and where there is a steep marginal slope you can expect deep water in the margins. Points and promontories extending out into the pit betray the presence of gravel bars. Fishing off a point, where baits can be placed on the crest of the bar, or down the slopes either side, is a well proven ploy in fishing for gravel pit tench. Visual evidence of this type has to be backed up by contour mapping, and there are two ways to go about it if you do not have access to a boat.

The first, to very quickly locate the shallowest bar in your swim, is to set up a large, buoyant sliding float, with a lead heavy enough not only to sink the float but also allow easy casting to maximum range. I set the float fairly shallow initially, obviously at the shallowest depth I expect to find, and cast to maximum range, aiming for an easily recognisable horizon feature, so that the cast can be reproduced. Bear in mind that this feature should be one still obvious in the dark, such as tall trees. There is no point aiming at something at water level that is impossible to see at night. It is most likely that the float will initially disappear from sight. Then begin a slow retrieve, taking in a few feet of line at a time, but periodically allowing a little slack off the reel to enable the slider to work properly. This technique will find any areas that are shallower than the depth setting, as the float will suddenly pop up. Let's say that initial setting was three feet.

Assuming that no area shallower than three feet has been located, I move the stop knot to four feet and repeat the procedure, casting at the same focal point. Using this progressive searching technique, you can quite quickly establish at least the major depth changes in front of you. In a swim of average width, I would generally cast out on three lines, one dead centre and two fanwise casts, one to the left and one right.

Once an interesting area has been located, you can find out more about it by leaving the float where it is and casting around it with a second rod, armed with its own slider. The first float aids casting accuracy and it is straightforward to investigate the adjacent contours thoroughly. In a swim containing several features, you may want to leave one or more permanent markers in place for a session, and the way to do this is simple. Having located the feature you wish to mark, cast out a second rod so that the float is marking the same feature. Retrieve the first tackle and then cut the line a foot above the stop knot. Form a loop in the free end and a similar loop in the end of the reel line. Tie the two loops firmly together with PVA string and then cast out again normally, using the dummy float as the casting target. After a couple of minutes, the PVA dissolves, leaving a permanent marker behind. At the end of the day, I retrieve markers with a grapple made out of a heavy lead and a large treble hook. The above technique is the one I prefer for locating possibly quite narrow bars running parallel to the bank, such as those I found at Deans Farm in the eighties. The crests of those bars were rarely more than two feet across and could be easily missed by more hit and miss mapping. For more general areas of interest, and ones of larger extent, such as a gradual drop off into deeper water over several yards, the mapping technique used widely by carp anglers is perfectly adequate. Specialist marker floats are tied to the end of the reel line, with a heavy lead link set on a wide bore run ring free to slide above the float. This should be held away from the float for at least a few inches to avoid the free running qualities being compromised by bottom weed fouling. I always start with the lead link a foot above the float.

There are a few important tips to get the best out of those specialist marker floats. First, it is important to use braid so that you can feel every little sensation. I do not use braid for my general fishing but for feature finding it is essential, not for finding the depth changes but for assessing the bottom composition. Second, use the most buoyant and highly visible float you can, coupled with at least two ounces of lead. One of those special bobbled leads will assist in recognising the bottom composition.

Having cast into position, steadily wind the float down until the line is taut. You can now understand why a heavy lead is essential; you want it to tell you when all the slack has been taken up. Now, pull off line from the reel spool a measured amount each time, say a foot, until the float appears on the surface. You now know the depth at that point, not forgetting the additional foot. Now progressively wind back the float towards you, repeating the process as often as you deem necessary. In a very short while, you will have established what depth variations exist between you and the furthest point of the cast.

To assess the bottom composition, I pull back steadily and smoothly to one side, with the rod horizontal, not vertical. I find it much better to make a sweeping backwards pull rather than winding the line back. The feel of fine gravel is unmistakeable, with the rod top emitting a gentle "bobble bobble" sensation. Coarser gravel is similar, but the bobbles are much more pronounced. If you are crossing smooth, hard silt, the retrieve feels easy and silky smooth, with no resistance. If the retrieve is smooth after initial light resistance, you have found softer silt or mud. A smooth retrieve with occasional short jags indicates small clumps of weed, whereas if the rod regularly becomes totally locked up and requires effort to get moving again, you are in thick weed. Although this all sound complicated in writing, a few practice casts will soon get you used to the differences in feel.

<u>Superb gravel pit fish of 8lb 4ozs</u>

Having said all that, on most gravel pits, if you only ever fished the shallow margins you would catch plenty of big tench. Most gravel pits have a marginal weed fringe and a narrow band of fairly shallow water, before dropping off into the main body of the pit. Tench love such areas and yet most gravel pit tench anglers seem obsessed with casting over the horizon.

2/ Estate Lakes, Reservoirs and Ponds

These waters give us the more traditional type of tench fishing, in that they are often far weedier and more overgrown than the majority of gravel pits, which can at times appear barren and inhospitable. Some large reservoirs can appear similar, the main difference being that they will be generally of more even bottom contours than most pits, the tench therefore being more evenly dispersed. Having said that, any naturally occurring features, such as hollows, shallows and feeder stream beds will always be worth investigating. Like tench everywhere, reservoir tench also have great affinity for weedbeds and searching for them in the proximity of lilies, rushes or potamogeton, for instance, will pay dividends.

If weed in a uniform reservoir is confined solely to bottom weed then the tench quite literally could be anywhere, and you will be advised to create your own hot spot by a combination of weed clearance techniques and pre-baiting.

Shallow, weedy estate and park lakes, and the small overgrown farm pond type of water, are where possibly the most interesting tench fishing is to be had, although it is a fact that the average size fish rarely compares with that from gravel pits and water supply reservoirs. In these waters, usually mud or silt bottomed, tench have a strong affinity for bulrushes and lilies, and will not be far away from them. In such soft bottomed environments, tench betray their presence in a variety of ways. Feeding tench colour the water rapidly. Find an area of muddiness in an otherwise clear lake and the chances are you have found tench. They also love to browse through marginal rushes and a sure give away is shaking of the stems as the tench force their way through them. The most distinctive sign, however, is those masses of tiny, needle bubbles, leading to that frothy fizz on the surface that is totally unmistakable. To me, that is still one of the most exciting sights in angling.

In stream fed estate lakes and those reservoirs created by damning stream valleys, the original stream bed is always a reliable spot for most species, tench included. Often, the only natural gravel will be found there, the bed is invariably deeper than the surrounding water and in a hot, dry summer the stream will be carrying dissolved oxygen which could be in short supply in the main body of the water. I remember the summer of 1993 on a local reservoir in very hot conditions, when I had several bumper bags of big tench fishing to just such a feature. A forty yard cast saw me in six feet of water over clean, fine gravel whereas either side of the feature was four feet deep and thick with blanket weed. Especially on reservoirs, it is well worth obtaining a map of the water's topography to see what route the stream follows through the water. If the stream veers within casting distance of the bank at any point, that would be a worthwhile place to start your campaign.

Rivers

I first became aware of tench in the river Great Ouse way back in the sixties when I had a handful of fish to four pounds when freelining lobs for summer chub, and a couple accidentally on crust in the winter, but never took them seriously enough to deliberately target them. And then, in 2001, I had several on successive barbel trips that really whetted my appetite. There is one particular barbel stretch I love fishing all night in summer for barbel, and I've had quite a few fabulous sessions in the dark hours. Generally, it was a case of baiting up in early afternoon, start fishing in early evening and through till dawn, when I made

<u>A prolific Great Ouse tench swim</u>

tracks for home. This particular night, I got chatting to another angler who said that he'd recently found that the chub and barbel had suddenly stopped biting at night, but were coming in the first two hours of daylight. By a strange coincidence, that night was very quiet until about two hours before dawn, when I missed three apparently unmissable pulls. By dawn, I was still fishless and, although tired, decided to stay on a couple of hours and test what the angler had said. No sooner was it fully light than I had another strong pull, but this time I connected. For a while, I wasn't sure what I'd hooked, and eventually I was amazed to see a good tench in the net, a fish that proved to weigh 6lb 2ozs. In the next hour it was all go, with another tench of 6lb 4ozs, plus chub of 5lb 3ozs and 5lb 5ozs. After that the swim died and, almost out on my feet, I headed for home.

The next time I visited the stretch, two weeks later, I had a good night with the chub and barbel, and then moved swims to where I'd previously caught the tench. In the first three hours of daylight I had no less than six solid thumps, which produced five tench and a chub. They certainly weren't monsters, with only two over five pounds, but with the biggest being only a whisker under 7lb it was becoming much more interesting. I was soon to discover that adjacent stretches to the one I'd been fishing had produced several tench over 8lbs with the

biggest known to be genuine being 9lb 5oz. That is a colossal tench anywhere but very special indeed from flowing water. My enthusiasm was well and truly kindled!

Swim location for river carp applies equally to tench, especially finding those areas with heavy marginal rushes and extensive cabbage patches. Where they do differ from carp is that I've had a fair few fish from quite streamy water, which you would feel more suited to chub and barbel. Conversely, the big bays I love for carping have never been productive for tench, although they certainly look the part.

The most productive tench swims I've found are quite small clearings in cabbages or little bays in rushes and, very much like perch, the closer the bait can be fished to the foliage the greater the chance of sport. Much of my summer overnight fishing on the upper Ouse is with both tench and carp in mind and it's quite interesting how it is usually only carp that fall to baits fished in both the more open water as well as the overgrown areas. Tench definitely prefer the security of cover. The two species co-exist very happily in the same environment, as they do in still waters.

One of the most critical aspects of river tenching in cabbages is that the bait must be presented close to the pads to have the best chance of bites. One of my favourite Ouse stretches features extensive cabbages along the far bank, which extend around three yards from the bank itself, with occasional seductive little bays. To fish those bays most effectively, I've found I have to present my baits within inches of the pads. In that, they share their affinity for cover with small stream summer perch. When I'm fishing this area, I fish clipped up, so that I know that every single cast will be right on the money.

Swim Preparation

All my river tench fishing has taken place on the middle to upper Great Ouse, and I've found that they are not nomadic in the way that carp are. Good swims remain so season after season, meaning that long term prebaiting, although never harmful, is not so vital to success. Knowing where the fish are is a tremendous starting point obviously. The other major difference between tench and carp is that I've found small river carp to be most reliably caught in the dark hours. If you have only one day available, you need to be on the bank very early to allow loose feeding for several hours before introducing a hook bait in the evening. By contrast, the overwhelming majority of my small stream tench, possibly as high as 95%, have come at dawn or in the two or three hours after. I can then be a lot more leisurely in arriving the afternoon before the planned dawn session, introducing the loose feed well before dark for the tench to home in on at dawn.

Whereas, if I am solely after carp, I tend to stick to boilies as bait and loose feed, I like more of a bait bed for tench to get their heads down on. Although I will still have a boilie on one hair, it will be accompanied by a method ball containing mixed goodies such as hemp, corn, small halibut pellets and stewed wheat. Stewed wheat is largely out of fashion these days, but it really is a superb feed ingredient for tench and bream especially. When I'm carp fishing with large boilies, using strong tackle, I don't want to be interrupted by bream, but the tenching is different. Using lighter tench rods, I am prepared to tolerate bream amongst my tench. In fact, over the last two summers on the upper Ouse, bream have been approaching double figures and make a welcome bonus in their own right.

Typical pristine Ouse tench

My initial feed for a tench swim would now be around 50 14mm boilies, and I've found Pallatrax Crustacean brilliant for tench, plus several balls of groundbait and a scattering of loose boilie paste samples. Hook baits initially will be paste wrapped boilies on short hairs, but if signal crayfish get on the case, even the boilies are not spared and I've got over that very successfully by reverting to popped up rubber corn. Over the last two summers Alan Lawrence and I have shared several two day and night sessions on the Ouse, often taking a number of very good tench and bream on the first night on boilies. The common scenario, however, was that the crayfish moved on to the feed on the second night, necessitating both of us switching to popped up rubber corn. Thereafter, all problems with the crays ceased and we had several nice tench and bream apiece.

Hard fighting Ouse male tench of just under 6lbs

Prebaiting

Baiting Techniques
One of the most important considerations with consistently successful tenching is baiting, both prior to the fishing session and on the day itself. There are limitless permutations as to what ingredients to use in our free feed, and the principle I always work to is that the feed should contain sufficient particles to keep the tench in the swim, foraging for them. Particles used consistently include maggots, casters, sweet corn, stewed wheat and hempseed, although there are dozens of others you can try. A well proven standard is a combination of maggots, casters and hemp in a base of fine brown breadcrumbs, either plain or flavoured.

If you are lucky enough to have access to a lightly fished water, one of the easiest and most devastating techniques is to use chopped lobs in plain breadcrumbs. I caught several large bags of TC tench in the early days on this simple approach. Hookbait was a large lobworm, which raises another interesting point. Just because you have baited with cereal plus small particles does not mean you cannot fish a large hook bait over it. At TC, I had several good bags of fish on large pieces of flavoured flake fished over carpets of hemp and casters.

__Mixed particles including casters, hemp, dead maggots, corn, squabs plus molasses__

With the advent of the Spomb, I can introduce particle feed easily up to about sixty yards. Very rarely will I be fishing for tench at longer range, but if I did need to introduce particles at extreme range my Microcat would be pressed into service. For long range work with traditional cereal based groundbait, the feed needs to be stiff enough to form regular balls that will catapult without breaking in flight, but that will dissolve easily into a fine carpet after settling on the bottom. Having said that, it is quick and easy to cast groundbait balls with a purpose made angler's slingshot. The balls need to be no more than about tangerine size and as well as being nice and firm need to be quite dry to avoid sticking to the sling. Get it right, and you can easily propel the bait eighty or ninety yards.

For catapulting or casting balls of bait a fair distance, which of necessity will demand stiffer bait than we would like, a good ploy is to poke a small hole in the side of each ball and fill it with a little dry sausage rusk, available from any butcher. As soon as rusk gets damp, it swells enormously and literally blows a ball of feed apart after a few minutes immersion in the water.

Most particles can be successfully incorporated in balls of feed for catapulting but the exception is large maggots. Their wriggling constantly breaks up the balls of feed, leading to scattering of bait all over the place, exactly what is not wanted. Alternatively, squatts or pinkies can be incorporated in balls of bait, as they are much less active, the larger hook maggots being reserved for the feeders. However, these days I only use dead maggots in the free feed, which I've found just as effective. I also like the feeder being the only source of live grubs. With the maggots only available in a tight cluster around my feeders, they act as focal points. In recent seasons, I have found the average size of tench to be much higher to this approach. I do not really have any definitive answer why this should be, but my results certainly bear it out. Perhaps scattering a large quantity of live maggots across a wide area over-stimulates the smaller, more aggressive males.

The quantity of feed to use has always been tricky to ascertain and my experiences in recent seasons has led me to a conclusion that, in hindsight, seems blindingly obvious. First, if you are able to prebait more than two days before the actual fishing session, a large quantity of bait is very effective and attracts a lot of tench into the swim. However, in the more common scenario of only being able to bait on the morning of arrival, or possibly the evening before, heavy baiting, especially with cereal based feeds, often has a temporarily negative effect. My records from two excellent tench summers of the 90s show that when I baited heavily on arrival for my normal two day session, my results were invariably poor on the first day. I also noted how often it was that fellow anglers moved into my swim after I left and in the two days that followed had far better catches than I had managed. Initially, I put this down to luck or bad angling on my part, but, as it became a pattern, I realised that there was more to it than that.

The classic combination, hemp and casters

So I changed the approach, to baiting initially with two pints of casters, a couple of handfuls of small halibut pellets and a pint of hemp scattered over the swim. Cereal feed was eliminated entirely. A further pint of casters went in each evening and the second morning. The difference this made was remarkable, with tench coming steadily from about two hours after the initial baiting. I never looked back after that, and caught tench consistently for the rest of the summer. What I believe happens is that, following the initial baiting, tench begin to drift into the swim in ones and twos and that it appears to take 24 to 36 hours before the swim is heavily colonised. With a very large quantity of bait available, the odds against a hookbait being taken early are therefore high, only improving slowly as the tench population builds up.

With much lighter baiting, in my case with casters, pellets and hemp, the hookbait of feeder fished maggots is most likely to attract any tench quickly, as they are not available anywhere else. The well scattered mixed small food items keep tench rooting around the swim, with the feeder providing a natural focal point. Also, while giving the short term benefit while the tench population is low, regular accurate casting to the same spot slowly builds up the bed of bait, leading to polarisation of more and more tench as the hours pass.

I have now adopted this approach as my standard tench tactic as it is very rare that I can prebait for several days. It is the approach I strongly recommend for those contemplating tenching in early spring. With water temperatures not yet at 'traditional' tench levels, it obviously pays to be slightly more cautious with baiting programmes. It is easy to introduce more bait as circumstances demand, but if you have committed too much in the first place and effectively killed the swim for a couple of days, you can't take it out again.

To précis then, as this book is concerned with the tactics to target the bigger tench, I tend to avoid the traditional approach of presenting a bait over a large bed of cereal feed for my normal two day sessions. When targeting the big females, my loose feed, as I've said, is based around a mixture of hemp, mini halibut pellets and casters. If I have any maggots left over from previous sessions, they will have been frozen and they can now be added to the mix. I like to scatter this feed over the swim rather than striving for a concentrated bed of goodies. The thinking is that the scattered nature of the bait bed reduces the alarm factor for the big females and, at the same time, encourages them to remain in the area constantly, while they forage around for the widely spread titbits.

Hookbaits

Maggots & Casters
As you will infer from the above, my tenching in recent years has been almost exclusively feeder work with maggot hookbaits, in conjunction with particle based loose feed. I am a great believer in flavouring maggots, having had dozens of experiences for both tench and roach that flavoured grubs have easily out caught plain ones in identical outfits fished side by side. My diaries show some quite dramatic examples; I'll just quote three from my tenching. In the eighties, pineapple flavouring took seven tench while I blanked on the plain bait. In the early nineties, vanilla flavouring resulted in a nine fish catch as opposed to one on the other rod. And in the late nineties, I took no less than 26 tench one day on vanilla, while only two fish came on the other outfit. I do like the confectionary flavours for tench and over the years I've had other decent catches on pineapple and vanilla, as well as slightly less dramatic results on tutti frutti, strawberry, scopex and maple cream.

I've also had success with maggots treated with liquid molasses, such that they become buoyant. The latter is a bait additive I can heartily recommend, especially if you do decide to use cereal groundbaits. Don't bother with the expensive powdered stuff, unless you're using it in your boilies. For tench groundbait, buy the gallon containers of pure molasses from horse and cattle feed suppliers and use it at about the rate of a cupful per five pounds of dry crumb. What I do is thoroughly mix the molasses with water and then add slowly to the dry ingredients until the mix is just right. It is almost impossible to make a bad mix with a water/molasses mixture. Although, as I've said, I rarely use large amounts of cereal for my tenching these days, I am increasingly combining my feeder fishing with a method mix approach. I mould a ball of Pallatrax Bloodworm method mix around the filled blockend. Not only does that slow down the release of the maggots it also creates a very attractive, sweet smell in the vicinity of the hook bait.

The most obvious drawback to maggots as a serious tench bait is the cost. You can minimise this somewhat by freezing any unused bait for the next trip, as they are just as effective an attractant as loose feed as live ones, and you will not need so many. Obviously, they can't crawl away. I freeze them simply by putting them into a sealable sandwich type bag, squeezing out as much of the air as possible, and then putting them in the freezer. That way, they retain their shape when thawed. I have tried killing them by the old boiling water technique, but they end up stretched and unattractive.

There has been a lot of discussion on the appeal or otherwise of coloured maggots, some anglers swearing by bronze, others by red and others who say it makes no difference whatever. In my case, I did have an experience at Horseshoe Lake a few years back where red maggots out caught the plain ones quite significantly. Ever since then, I've used reds exclusively in my tenching. I still don't know whether it makes the slightest difference and whether that particular catch was just a fluke. But, I fish with more confidence and as I catch my share of tench the red maggots are obviously not proving detrimental.

One of the best tench baits of all are casters, and they always figure prominently in my free feed when still water tench fishing with feeders. Because of their delicate nature, I rarely use real casters as actual hook baits, using instead two or three Enterprise rubber artificials. One of the best tench anglers I know is my old mate Chris Turnbull and I know that Chris really rates rubber casters as highly as I do.

Boilies & Pastes

Although my experience of using boilies for tenching is comparatively sketchy, I do know that they are awesome tench baits. They are also useful for those anglers like me who are interested in the very biggest fish. Specialist boiled baits can be used to target bigger than average tench, just as they can for chub and barbel. In recent years, I have done a lot of river carping on the upper to middle Great Ouse, which also has a healthy tench population. Most of that fishing has been with 14mm Pallatrax boilies, mainly with Crustacean Cocktail or Multiworm Cocktail. The tench simply love them. It is perhaps surprising then that I have done so little still water tenching using boilies. My excuse is simple enough. I just love tenching with maggots or casters, still the most effective technique in my book.

But what I perhaps lack in boilie experience I make up for with experience of soft flavoured pastes of various pedigrees. Sweet flavours have worked well, although I admit to having used savoury flavours far less, so the comparisons are a little unfair. Of all the pastes I have used, the ones that have given me the best results are, in order of results, sweet almond, sweet caramel, maple cream and tutti frutti. Almond in particular is a great tench attractor, although I have found it mediocre for all other species. I have also found, strangely enough, that almond gives very indifferent results when used with maggots. Why a flavour should be great in pastes and poor on maggots is illogical, but one of those strange facts that makes angling the fascinating pastime it is.

Lovely fish to rubber corn/strawberry squab cocktail

Baits I really rate for tench are the pillow shaped Pallatrax Squabs. They are available in several confectionary flavours and various colours and I particularly like the red strawberry. I've had a fair few tench and bream on those, when little rudd have made even rubber maggots a nightmare to use. Away from the confectionary flavours, one of the greatest Pallatrax carp baits is Jungle and I can confirm that tench love the Jungle Squabs. On the bottom lake at Acton a few years ago, I had fifteen tench in a carp session on Jungle. They just wouldn't leave me alone!

Lobworms & Redworms

Lobs are terrific tench baits, especially in early summer, and although I favour the feeder approach for gravel pits, the humble lob is always my first choice if I'm tenching a weedy estate lake. This is especially true if I'm lift float fishing in early season, when tench gallop away merrily with large baits. By mid to late July you often find the bites getting a littler more circumspect and then it may be time to reduce the hook size and switch to a redworm or dendrobaena. At the time of writing, July 2013, I have only just started using dendrobaenas and they are a terrific bait. I've just had a string of good fish on cocktail hookbaits of two of these worms with two red maggots mounted on size 8 hooks. The bites have been wonderful sail away affairs.

When you see tench creating that unmistakeable Alka Seltzer like fizz near to weed beds, it's a good chance that they're feeding over bloodworm colonies. In these circumstances, dendrobaenas or redworms have a good chance of being accepted greedily. If you decide to use a full sized lobworm, its pulling power can be enhanced by air injecting it at one end with a syringe kept especially for the purpose. A large lob requires a bigger hook than does a redworm and the air injection helps to counterbalance the heavier hook somewhat as well as making part of the worm waver enticingly off bottom. Needless to say, when using a syringe to inject air in this way, do the job on the lid of a bait box or similar. Do not hold the bait in your hands. You do not want to inject yourself accidentally and create an air embolism, which can be fatal.

Although I said earlier that I generally favour the feeder approach with small hooks on gravel pits, if you have access to a pit which has been very lightly fished, the traditional large bait approach can work very well. I've already mentioned the early days at TC pit when Trefor and I were among only a handful of anglers fishing, and we caught a staggering number of big tench on lobs or flavoured pastes on size 6 hooks. As soon as the water became busy, however, and maggots began to be introduced in large quantities, the big bait approach became progressively less effective.

Bread

As with most species these days, bread in all its forms has become a much neglected tench bait. I confess that I am as guilty as others in this regard, but there is no doubt that it can be highly effective in the right circumstances. In my experience, these circumstances are principally on lightly fished intimate and weedy waters such as small ponds, canals or estate lakes. Where it is not so effective is on those pressured waters which have been given either the maggot or boilie treatment.

On the odd occasion when I fish the traditional tench method of the lift float at dawn alongside lilies, nothing beats a nice fluffy piece of flake, unless it is a lobworm. Where there is a thin layer of bottom weed, a piece of anchored crust an inch or two off bottom is as appealing to a big tench as it is to a winter chub. Flavoured baits also work well. I have caught good tench on baits dipped in honey and, as with pastes, flake or crust doused in almond flavour works well.

An interesting option when you want to present a critically balanced bait is to treat a piece of crust with just sufficient paste added to just make it sink. Just as with the special pastes discussed earlier, a cheap and cheerful alternative is to make yellow bread paste with custard powder and a little almond flavour. This can be used on its own as a simple bottom bait or added to crust for the balanced option.

There is no other bait that can mimic the unique texture of breadflake or breadcrust. If you find yourself in a situation where there are tench in the marginal shallows, a good piece of weightless, slow sinking squeezed flake is often irresistible to a big tench.

Simple Pastes

My definition of a simple paste is one that can be concocted cheaply from everyday ingredients available from supermarkets, as opposed to the more specialised and more expensive baits requiring boilie base mixes.

The first classic is sausage meat paste, originally produced with barbel in mind but which quickly proved effective for both carp and tench. The sausage paste was made by mixing unskinned sausage meat with a binding agent such as fine breadcrumbs, biscuit meal or finely ground dry pet foods. Spicing the basic paste with a little curry powder has proved very effective for carp, chub and barbel and I have no doubt whatever that it would be equally as effective if I gave it a concerted trial fore tench.

As well as sausage meat paste, other glutinous food stuffs can be made into usable pastes, and one of the best of these is tinned tuna, which most fish adore. Although I never used this particular bait myself, a friend had several good carp and tench on tuna made into a stiff paste using crumbled Weetabix.

Is it possible to produce an excellent paste using an appealing dry ingredient, and the most successful I ever used for tench was based on powdered Trout Fry Crumb. Obviously, a dry powder needs a glutinous content to make a usable paste, and I used actual gluten. My original bait was a mixture of trout fry crumb, baby milk and sufficient water to make a stiff paste, but a massive improvement to the bait was made by substituting eggs for the water. The eggs gave the exterior of the paste a lovely sheen and a very waxy texture which the fish obviously found very appealing.

Several different flavours caught me tench, but the best by far was the first I tried, which was almond. I had the biggest catch of TC tench I ever saw on that bait. When using a flavoured paste as hook bait, I usually laced my free feed with the same flavour. With the almond paste, I remember, I was using groundbait of pure breadcrumbs, containing chopped lobs with a few maggots, coloured yellow and flavoured with almond essence. The problem with flavoured baits is that they do seem to blow quite quickly and you must keep an open mind to keep modifications going if catches start to falter. Knowing what I know now about designer barbel baits, and how they blow if over flavoured, it could be that my early tench baits suffered from the same problem. If I get into flavoured tench pastes again, I will be much more sparing with the flavour levels.

The one basic paste I've never tempted a tench with is the chub classic, cheese paste, although I've tried it several times on days when the tench were certainly feeding.

Sweetcorn

Sweetcorn is a terrific tench bait, either in the natural yellow form or any of the coloured and flavoured varieties. I particularly rate the red strawberry variety although I do fondly recall a good number of tench that accepted banana flavoured corn at Orchid during a carp session. Red strawberry corn/red maggot cocktails accounted for my largest catch of Horseshoe tench a few years back. With tench, it's a mistake to overdo the loose feeding with corn, especially the natural yellow variety. As with barbel, I've found that large beds of the stuff do make the fish spooky. It is more effective being used sparingly, as little titbits among the main mass of feed. Corn always figures in my prebaiting, and a large bucket of hemp or mixed particles will never hold more than two tins of corn.

Wheat

One of the most underused baits of all must be wheat, stewed slowly until the husk splits to reveal the creamy white interior. Stewed wheat is an absolutely lethal bait for roach, but it is also loved by tench and bream and for that reason always figures in my base feed. As with sweetcorn, it is wise to use stewed wheat sparingly, but for a different reason. It is dense and very filling. As a hook bait, it is quite difficult to use at any kind of range as it is quite delicate but where you are fishing close in, say under a lift float, it comes into its own. As I describe in the section on using the lift float, big baits like lobs are fished with a tail of around eight inches on the bottom. But when bites start becoming finicky, reducing the tail to just an inch or two with a small bait will often pay dividends. A compact, dense bait like wheat on a small hook is then ideal and I've had some nice fish that way. As an aside, this short tail lift float and wheat combination is deadly for margin feeding crucians.

Artificial Baits

Over the last few seasons I've been totally converted to rubber baits for tenching. When I'm maggot fishing now, the hook bait is invariably two red Enterprise rubber maggots on a short hair. I prefer to bottom fish tench baits but if I have bottom weed to contend with I switch to the buoyant version and fish a popped up bait. The same goes for caster fishing and I know that many specialist tench anglers only use two or three buoyant casters for the species.

Popped up rubber red maggots with a little red rig foam for increased buoyancy

On the Ouse, I've had dozens of good tench on two grains of popped up rubber corn, usually when I've been forced to switch from boilies because of the attention of crayfish. Where loose feeding is with hemp and corn, two yellow grains fished to hover just off bottom is very eye catching. With more and more still waters also now infested with crayfish, rubber baits are an absolute godsend when effective angling would otherwise be near on impossible.

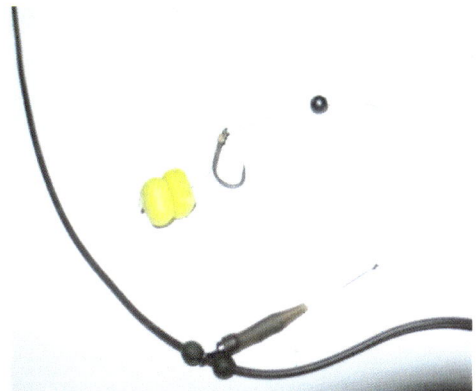

Popped up rubber corn

Fairly new in my fishing are rubber worms, especially redworms. These are great in cocktail baits and two favourite offerings are redworm/maggot and redworm/corn. I have also just started to use Enterprise artificial boilies. They are buoyant baits for fishing popped up but are cleverly designed with a small hole so that they can have small amounts of tungsten putty inserted for either a true bottom bait or one that is critically balanced. I am using the natural brown on the Ouse, to match my Pallatrax Crustacean Cocktail feed baits, in both 12mm and 15mm.
The main problem to overcome when moving to artificial baits is one of confidence and it took me a long time to get over the conviction that I had to have at least one real bait on the hook. A session at Horseshoe, however, when bottom weed was a nightmare, cured me of my reticence. I had fifteen good tench on three popped up maggots, fished six inches off bottom. All the bites were absolute screamers and since then I've had dozens of fish of all species on rubber baits. The obvious and important benefit is their resistance to destruction by small fish, especially with caster fishing.

Dried Naturals
I have included this short section because the Naturals that Simon Pomeroy of Pallatrax has launched are proving deadly for many species and especially tench. Among the small hookbaits available are tinned bloodworm, daphnia, silkworm, river shrimp, water snails and giant mealworms I particularly rate these as additions to method mixes. Also available are the same products dried and ground, and these are obviously specifically intended to enhance groundbaits and method mixes. Ground dried earthworm is also available for the same purpose.

What really excites me is the newly launched Hydra range of dehydrated snails and mussels. There are four products available, small snails, brown snails, black snails and water mussels. To use them, simply immerse in water for a while or flavoured water if that takes your fancy, and they then re-hydrate into soft and usable naturally occurring baits. I am just getting into these myself and early results with tench and bream are very exciting.

Lovely Ouse seven pounder

Methods & Tactics

1/ Float Fishing

Under this heading will come traditional laying on methods and variations on the lift method. On a lightly fished water, I like to fish large baits such as lobs or flake under a simple quill cocked by one large shot. With the shot resting on the bottom and the rod in the rest, the line is drawn tight enough so that the float is at half cock. When tench are feeding confidently, most of the bites are signified by the float falling flat as the shot is lifted, or by it moving rapidly across the surface. With large baits, this laying on method will normally see the shot at least eight inches from the hook bait.

When float fishing on a summer morning on an estate lake, the bites will usually become progressively more finicky as the morning wears on. Rather than really positive indications you now may get all sorts of annoying little lifts and trembles, which take ages to develop into strikable bites, if they develop at all. This is the time to fish the lift method. For close in work, the same float can be employed, but now I would move the shot to within an inch of the hook and swap the large hook for a much smaller pattern and bait with a correspondingly smaller bait. One example could be switching from a full sized lob on a size 6 to a redworm, grain of corn or wheat, on a 14.

Where close range fishing allows the use of the quill cocked by one shot, the principle is simple. With the shot only an inch from the hook, set the float slightly over depth and cast a little beyond the baited area. Now submerge the rod top and draw the tackle to the fishing area. This makes sufficient angle in the line to compensate for the over depth and the float just cocks under tension, telling you the shot is on the bottom. Then place the rod in two rests and draw the line tight until only about the top inch of the float is visible. With this setting, the tackle is sensitive to the tiniest of movements of the bait. A tench has only to lift the bait an inch for the float to shoot up in the water, giving a very dramatic indication. Lift float fishing really is great fun and very effective.

At longer range, exactly the same principles can be applied, but you will obviously require far bigger floats with multiple shotting. The trick here is to make the tell tale shot sufficiently large that a good lift on the float is registered when that shot is lifted.

<u>Gorgeous fish of 7lb 12ozs</u>

Fishing the Swimfeeder

As I've said, my tenching over recent years has centred on the use of the feeder with maggot hookbaits, without doubt one of the most productive methods of catching tench. In the float fishing section, I outlined how tench in all water types usually take big baits confidently at dawn, but how bites often tail off quite quickly as the sun comes up. As we've seen, bites can become more finicky during the day, necessitating reducing bait size.

That principle is intrinsic in the efficiency of the maggot feeder approach to modern tenching, and means that catching tench is no longer primarily confined to the dawn period but can be enjoyed all day. The method is essentially universal; by that I mean that it will catch the avidly feeding fish at dawn, but still work equally well with the sun high in the sky.

The rig I now use for all my tenching is a mini helicopter arrangement, with a short hook link fished above either a Kamasan Black Cap feeder or a Stonze weight. First, I slide about two feet of quick sink 2mm tubing on to the main line, which in my case is 10lb Gamma, and then slide on to the tubing a rubber shock bead. You need the size that gives a tight interference fit on the rubber. I slide that well up the tubing and then put on a quick release speed swivel, before sliding on two more shock beads. These swivels have a normal eye at one end and an open hook at the other, over which is placed the loop of a hook link before trapping it under a tapered silicon sleeve. When changing hook links, it is only necessary to slide the silicon sleeve back, unhook the hooklink loop and replace with a fresh link. Changing hooklinks takes literally seconds. The swivel can now be trapped between the beads and positioned anywhere up the length of tubing. The reason for using two beads below the link is to resist the hooklink travelling down the main line on a hard cast. At the end of the line I put on a Pallatrax tulip bead and then a swivel carrying a snap link. This link will either carry a feeder or Stonze.

My standard helicopter rig with Kamasan Black Cap feeder

My hooklinks are usually 8lb Gamma fluorocarbon, which is very fine for its strength, between three and six inches in length. Hooks are usually sizes 10 to 16, eyed Pallatrax, which are exceptionally strong. Having tied on the hook I slide on one of the silicon sleeves and then tie in a simple figure of eight loop knot at the end of the link. Each of my hooklinks carries its own silicon sleeve, making hooklink changing even faster.

Whether I'm using a method ball approach around a Stonze or a feeder set up, I slide the hooklink so that the bait fishes adjacent to the loose feed, in typical method feeder application. One feature of the set up I like is what happens when you get a big tench on the end. A weakness of a fixed, above the lead or feeder arrangement is when playing a fish. The weight hanging down from the fish's mouth can either weaken the hook hold or can catch in bottom foliage leading to snagging. The beauty of my version is that the hooklink trapping beads on the tubing gently slide down to the tulip bead during the fight so that there is then no pendulum effect from the feeder or weight. I've yet to have a fish snagged with this rig. Lastly, in these politically correct days, the rig is ultra safe. If there is a main line break anywhere, the tubing slides off the line and two shock beads easily pull off the tubing. There is zero chance of a fish ever being tethered by either a heavy feeder or terminal weight.

Above rig with method ball encasing the feeder

I am happy with this set up in fairly weed free swims, but, in weedy water I usually change to a fine braided hooklink. For many years I used 10lb Sufix Herculine which is thinner than 3lb mono. Last season I used both 15lb ESP camo sink link and Pallatrax 15lb green braid and have been delighted with both. Both are extremely fine but of the two, the green braid is very slightly stiffer and less prone to tangling.

The problem with braids generally, of course, is tangling, and any rig you use is going to be prone to this, especially where regular long casting is involved. One way round the problem of tangling on the cast is to treat the hooklink with Kryston Super Stiff anti tangle gel. When retrieving for a recast using braided links, wind in very slowly. It is the retrieve that makes hooklinks spin, and the faster you wind in the more the problem is accentuated. With all the precautions in the world, though, fine braid links tangle badly occasionally on the retrieve, and when they do you change them. The rig I've described allows replacement of hooklinks in seconds. Having said all that, the helicopter rig described is the best I've ever used for minimising tangles. To reduce the risk even further, I now always wrap the hook in a piece of dissolving foam.

In tench fishing, as opposed to chub or barbel, I have had evidence over the years that the thickness of hook link material definitely influences the number of bites. Years ago, I initially thought that switching to lower diameter pre-stretched or double strength type monofilaments would provide the perfect answer. However, that flirtation was short lived. These materials have poor sudden shock resistance, with the result that they can create as many problems as they solve, breaking on the strike being an obvious example. Using them on a two day session, I remember losing several nice tench to sudden and unexplained breakages. Consequently, I abandoned these lines and now stick to fluorocarbon or fine braid, depending on fishing conditions.

Legering

This section is concerned with traditional legering for tench with single large baits. Obviously, a specific legering scenario is the use of the swimfeeder with maggots, as described above.

If I am presenting a large bait, a boilie say, I revert to a more orthodox leger rig with the hooklink below the feeder or terminal weight. In that regard, my tenching is nothing more than scaled down carp fishing.

The rig I use depends on the bottom composition and the presence or otherwise of weeds or deep, soft silt. On hard gravel beds, standard running legers are just as effective as they ever were. With no resistance from weed, a tench can easily take line through a large bore run ring without feeling anything amiss and this might make all the difference if the fish are in a finicky mood. With anything stopping free travel, a suspicious fish could drop the bait without giving a striking opportunity. We've all had those maddening twitches and trembles.

Years ago, like many anglers, I believed the answer lay in making things more and more resistance free or increasing hook links to ridiculous extremes. Occasionally those measures worked, but more often than not they didn't. What changed my thinking were my winters spent after reservoir roach. Using standard running feeder set ups, bites were invariably maddeningly inconclusive affairs, even to five foot hooklinks. It was only when I learned from roach angling friends that the way round the problem was to use short hook links, heavy feeders and heavy butt indicators. It sounded all wrong, but the bites then became real churners. Obviously, the roach were pricked quickly after mouthing the bait because of the short link, encountered a large resistance preventing bait ejection and bolted in panic. From a hooking ratio of about 25% on the running set up, it became 100% to the bolt rig arrangement.

Applying the same logic to my tench fishing has seen the occasions when I am frustrated by twitchy bites from tench almost a thing of the past. If I am using a bolt type of set up for larger baits, I always opt for the semi fixed option. I do need a system where the terminal weight will detach up the line under extreme pressure, especially when a big fish has charged off through blanket weed or similar. A totally fixed lead in this situation is possibly going to lead to completely irretrievable snagging. I compare this to feeder fishing for barbel in streamer. A fixed feeder is similarly risky, whereas one free to slide decreases the risk of losing a fish in the roots.

When not feeder fishing, I use just two variants on the semi fixed bolt rig. The first is for short range fishing, and is the one I use all the time on rivers. This incorporates an in-line Stonze weight mounted on a special sleeve. This sleeve has an interference fit. This is fished above hooklinks of between six and twelve inches depending on the bait and I almost always use the Stonze as a holder for a method ball. The shorter hook link will be used for baits such as corn or lobs, while the longer links are reserved where I am presenting boiled baits of 14mm or above.

Standard river rig. Semi fixed Stonze with braided hooklink

For long range, I incorporate a swivel Stonze mounted on a safety clip. I hasten to add that the clip is not so I can dump the weight when I hook a fish, a tactic I do not agree with. It is a convenient way to set up and one that can be left in place with the rod set up for the next session. All I have to do is assemble the rod, clip on the appropriate weight and off I go.

For most of my legering needs with bigger baits I stick with Pallatrax green braid for the hooklinks, alleviating tangles on the cast with a PVA stringer for boilies or a PVA bag for other baits. However, if I want to present a bait into a tight gap in weed I will switch to a short, 6" stiff link rather than soft braid. This obviously swivels away from the lead in a confined space where the braid tends either to collapse in an untidy heap on top of the weight or get hung up on the weed. The stiff link material I use is Pallatrax Snaglink, with just enough of the coating peeled off for the hair and about an inch up from the hook. This gives a little movement to a taking fish. Once again, extra security against weed interference is provided by a wrap of dissolving foam around the hook on the cast.

Hair Rigs

As with most of my specimen fishing these days, the use of the hair rig is almost universal in my tenching. Possibly the only time I use bait directly on a hook is if I'm fishing lobs. For fishing artificial maggots, casters and corn, which is featuring in a high percentage of my tench fishing these days, I prepare my hooklinks at home. I dispense with the normal hair rig needle and boilie stop arrangement and tie on the baits first with the hooklink braid. With the bait in place, I then tie on a hook with the knotless knot, making sure that the bait is away from the hook bend no more than half an inch. I prefer this system for rubber baits to either standard mounting with a hair rig needle or by supergluing because the danger of losing the baits is eliminated. I don't want tench or any other species pulling the baits off the hair and ingesting the rubber.

As for hair length, I do like to keep this short, no more than half an inch from the bend, because tench are very much browsing feeders. Carp will suck up baits from a fair distance whereas tench tend to hover over them. Long hairs make missing tench bites or hooking the fish on the outside of the mouth more likely than it is with carp.

A terrific application for the hair rig is the Medusa rig, for presenting a bait of many real maggots. For this, I mount a 12mm cork ball on a normal hair and then coat it with superglue. Hold the cork ball in a tub of maggots for half a minute and you end up with a writhing ball of a hookbait. I've had lots of tench to that approach. Incidentally it's also lethal for barbel.

Casting Accuracy

Earlier, I mentioned my approach to the bigger tench usually involved no free feeding with live maggots, but confined the use of live maggots to those in my feeders. The idea is to create a localised "hot spot". To maximise the benefit of this ploy, accurate casting is obviously vital, and I achieve this in one of two ways. Having decided upon my fishing range and having introduced my loose feed to suit, the terminal rigs are cast to the same spot, the line placed in the line clip on the reel, and then an insulating tape marker placed alongside the rod spigot. I buy white tape for this. When actually fishing, cast to the clip, and then obviously unclip the line while awaiting a bite and, hopefully, playing a big tench. For recasting, adjust the main line so that the tape marker is once again adjacent to the spigot, then clip up and retrieve. After landing a fish, before rebaiting, cast out the terminal rig, away from the swim, until you see the tape pass the spigot. Then position the tape as before, clip up, and off you go again.

This is the best method to use if you intend fishing the dark hours, but if you only fish in daylight for your tench, as I tend to these days, you may prefer to use a swim marker. Here's the simplest method of marking the right area. Using the marker float and a decent lead, cast around until you have found the area you intend fishing. Having done so, pull a few feet off the reel spool and then clip up and retrieve. Break off the float and lead about a foot above the float or float stop knot and tie in a loop in the end of the line. Tie a similar loop in the end of the main line and then tie the two loops together with PVA string. Now cast out hard enough for the line to tighten to the line clip, leave for a minute and retrieve, leaving the float in place in exactly the right place. To retrieve the marker at the end of the session, I use a special grapple consisting of a big sea lead and large treble. It's simple to cast alongside the marker, snag the line and retrieve. Obviously, if you're incapable of casting accurately, this is not the method for you!

Spring Tenching

Before I began seriously targeting tench in spring three seasons ago, I wouldn't have believed how voraciously the species can feed as soon as the first hint of warming in the water occurs. What appears to happen, certainly on the waters I've fished, is that they feed with real abandon through late March and April, becoming much more elusive from May onwards. If I look back at recent seasons, I have had some exceptional catches of fish throughout April, with fish to well over nine pounds. As the traditional tench season arrived in mid June, the fishing became harder and harder. That was from a quite barren gravel pit, but it was the same story at a reservoir I devoted some time to. Here again, catches of over a dozen fish were made in April but, by mid May, everyone was struggling for a bite. The first message, therefore, if you're looking forward to some spring tench fishing, is to start early; late March is not too soon.

<u>An early April eight pounder</u>

With a general lack of weed so early in the season, one of the first essentials is to locate areas where the chances of sport are going to be greatest and, as most of my spring tenching has been on gravel pits, I will confine my comments to these waters. The most reliable tench swim in my opinion is the crest of a shallow gravel bar, and this is particularly true when there is a lack of other features, especially weed beds. The main features in a weedless pit, of course, are the margins, which tench love at all times. So I don't want tench swims too far out either, and am always happiest when fishing at thirty yards or less. On one pit I fished for the first time a few years ago, I made the mistake of fishing a cracking looking bar 60 yards from the bank, but really struggled for bites. I could find no gravel bars closer in than that and have to admit that I was blinkered in my approach. I had developed a "fish a bar or nothing" mentality. And then I discovered that big tench were being caught sometimes only one rod length from the bank. After all my experience, that was a basic error.

So, if a pit is not well blessed with bars, or they are a long way out, I would no longer target them for early season tench, but concentrate on the marginal areas. Even in cold water, most pits have a marginal weed fringe and a narrow band of fairly shallow water, before dropping off into the main body of the pit. If you only ever fished these margins, you would catch a great many tench. Most of my best spring catches have been made at thirty yards range or less, in a maximum of four feet of water, as the bottom begins to drop away into much deeper water.

Tench Water Comparisons

During my many years chasing big tench, I've noticed important differences in the habits and behaviour of the fish between different water types. The three most important still water fisheries are gravel pits, reservoirs and estate lakes. Let's have a look first at the variants I've found on the first two of those.

Gravel Pits & Reservoirs

The first significant variable I've found between pit and reservoir tench is the effect of wind and weather. In reservoirs, cool, windy conditions have been found extremely productive for tench feeding generally. For instance, the 1993 and 1998 summers were very forgettable for sun worshippers, but reservoir tenching at the Midland reservoirs was outstanding. The water I was fishing at the time was blessed with strong winds, rain and mediocre temperatures for most of the summer, but some of my best catches came on the most dismal days, when everything was sodden and fishing conditions most uncomfortable.

A windswept spring day at a gravel pit known to hold huge tench

By contrast, in years of hot, calm conditions, the tench fishing has been much more difficult. Interestingly, these are precisely the conditions that have always given me excellent results on the gravel pits I have fished for tench.

Although I have found reservoir tench to be stimulated into feeding by wind, I have never found any evidence on these waters that the actual location of the tench has any link with wind direction. It seems that a good swim remains a good swim from whatever quarter the wind is blowing. The gravel pit tench of my acquaintance, however, like most gravel pit species, are much more nomadic than their reservoir or estate lake cousins. On pits, I have found a link to their location and a strong wind. A stiff onshore wind at TC pit was always a reliable indicator of tench location.

One area of uniformity between pit and reservoir tench is that neither water type is particularly productive after dark. In thirty years, the number of tench I have taken at night has been modest in relation to the hours fished. Were I only fishing for tench, I would long ago have given up night fishing but, of course, many waters also hold big roach, bream and carp, which are very viable after dark targets.

Please remember, however, the old adage that there are no such words as always and never in angling; an open mind is essential. In all the gravel pits I've fished, very few tench have come in the dark. However, I remember a month in the eighties at TC pit when I never caught a tench in daylight, but took thirty good fish at night, every one between 11.00pm to 2.00am. After that, it was back to normal. I didn't understand it then, and I still don't.

On reservoirs, if the dark hours are slow, that cannot be said for the dawn period. Where reservoir tenching is concerned, if you are not fishing at the crack of dawn, you risk missing the most productive time of the lot. Having said that, it can take a few hours for tench to really get their heads down over a newly introduced carpet of feed. An arrival at dawn, therefore, in a previously unbaited swim, is likely to see a couple of quiet hours before the fish move in. On a two-day session, I would expect tench bites to commence at dawn on the second day, whereas the first morning might not see the first bite until mid morning or beyond. It is obviously all to do with the build up of feed over the session.

Dawn at Hollowell reservoir

It is interesting that I have found exactly the same situation on gravel pits on two-day sessions. Many writers have stated that the dawn feeding period on gravel pits does not occur. That is exactly the opposite of my experience, as I've had dozens of good tench as the first light is appearing in the eastern sky.

Again, I will always remember at TC being told by two regulars that it was a waste of time fishing at dawn, as you never had any bites until mid morning. They never arrived until after 8.00 a.m. in all the summers I fished there, so how would they know! In the hours before they

arrived, I often filled my boots! As I said, keep an open mind.
I have also found the daytime fishing in reservoirs much as for pits, regular bites coming up to perhaps 2.00pm and then tailing off badly in the afternoon. What is interesting, though, on both water types, is that an extra big fish will often turn up as a single, out of the blue capture in late afternoon, perhaps to the first bite in hours.

Estate Lakes

I do tend to concentrate my tenching on gravel pits, the chances of fish into double figures being undeniably higher. However, that is not to say that estate lakes do not have the potential to throw up huge fish. I've had several nine pound plus tench from these "traditional" waters. The question I'm often asked is how I approach such a water for a very big tench and would that approach be much different from that I employ in pits. Just to recap, I've found a much higher average weight of tench in gravel pits results from a scattered particle feed with no loose maggots, using maggots in the feeder only as a focal point. Use of pints of loose maggots, as well as lots of cereal feed, tends to bring in hordes of smaller and more active male tench. For a session of two days or less, this can seriously reduce the chances of contacting a big nomadic female.

So, let's look at the essential differences between pits and these traditional tench waters. First, they are usually far weedier and more overgrown than the majority of pits, which can at times appear barren and inhospitable. Although any naturally occurring features, such as hollows, shallows and feeder stream beds will always be worth investigating, the weedbeds are the vital ingredient. Tench have great affinity for weedbeds and this factor alone ensures that tench in weedy ponds and lakes are much less nomadic than their gravel pit counterparts. For this reason, the baiting technique I outlined above is not so effective. When you're fishing for resident fish, rather than odd nomadic individuals looking for an opportunist meal, it's impossible to be size selective by loose feeding. The only approach is to catch as many tench as possible and hope the big one comes along. It is possible to be size selective by using huge designer boilies, but that's another topic altogether.

A productive estate lake

My baiting technique in estate lakes therefore has essential differences from my gravel pit approach. I still retain the principle that the feed should contain sufficient particles to keep the tench in the swim, foraging for them. Particles invariably include casters, corn, mini halibut pellets and hempseed. I still tend to restrict the use of live maggots, apart from my feeders, especially where there is an abundance of nuisance fish, especially small rudd and perch. On very weedy waters, one of the most devastating techniques is to incorporate chopped lobs.

I've had many great tench catches on the humble lobworm, these days a very under-used and under-rated bait. Fishing a large hookbait, such as a lobworm or generous chunk of bread flake, over a carpet of hemp and casters, is just as effective for tench as it is for barbel.

The most obvious difference in my preparation for lakes as opposed to pits is that I do incorporate cereal feed, and prefer open ended feeders rather than block ends. Generally, I start with a few Spombs of mix, and then top it up with regular recasting of my feeders. If tench are coming regularly, I will periodically put a couple more Spombs of mix in to boost the baiting rate. These days, my base mix consists of a mixture of finely ground Vitalin and Pallatrax method mix, sweetened with a generous dollop of liquid molasses during the mixing process. I also incorporate the juice out of the hemp and the liquid out of the corn in the mix; in fact it's not a bad ploy to liquidise a couple of tins of corn to produce a scattering of corn fragments through the bait carpet. For use in open ended feeders, I don't want the feed too wet or binding; it needs to be a fairly dry, crumbly consistency.

With the softer bottomed lakes, where generally there will be a larger head of tench of a smaller average size than in gravel pits, much more loose feed is required. For a two day session, I have used as much as ten kilos of cereal and several pints of particles initially, topping up every couple of hours during the session.

One of the most obvious differences between the tenching on gravel pits and that of weedy lakes is in the feeding times. On every water I've fished, of whatever type, dawn has always been a good time. However, other tench anglers I respect have stated that, on their pits, dawn is often poor. By contrast, the middle of the day and early afternoon, even in blazing sunshine, can give brilliant sport. I've also had a lot of good fish in the heat of the day, from 11.00am until 3.00pm. Things are much different on traditional estate lakes. Here we get the more classic tenching, with needle bubbles rising around the lilies at dawn as the tench begin feeding in earnest. On a hot summer's day, just as our gravel pit fish are really coming on the feed, say in late morning, the sport in our estate lake will very often be coming to an end. You really have to be an early riser to get the best out of lake tench, but this is not so vital on pits. Don't ask me why there is this difference, because I haven't a clue!

Setting the bobbins at an Oxford pit

Care and Conservation

While not as fragile as bream or barbel, tench deserve the same respect as all other fish and it is expected that all anglers do all they can to minimise damage to this most magnificent of fish. Tench can be very active on the bank, especially the feisty males, and you should always include in your kit a well padded unhooking mat. Remember, the very biggest fish are found in gravel pits and rough gravel does not make a kind resting place for any fish, including tench. I also have a large weigh sling for carrying the fish back to the water's edge. I have witnessed far too many fish being dropped as they were carried back to the water after a photographic session.

It has been many years since I last used a carp sack, for any fish. In a warm summer, I'm never altogether happy with fish in sacks. I now stop fishing and take any photographs I need there and then, setting up the camera equipment while the fish safely reposes in the landing net. With modern cameras, especially models such as my Canon G6 which features a flip around screen, self portraiture is a doddle, even in the middle of the night. If a photo is required, with the fish still safely in the net, I set up my tripod and camera, set the distance, check the camera settings and often take one test shot. Once I'm happy with the set up, the net mesh is laid on the mat by my knees and I can take half a dozen self portraits in less than thirty seconds. There is no need to have the fish out of water longer than that and all the big fish I catch return as fit and strong as when I first hooked them.

When playing tench, use the tackle strength at your disposal and do not allow the fish to fight itself to the point of exhaustion. It is preferable to pressure it into the net as soon as possible, within reason. This is far better achieved by playing a big fish using a properly set clutch than it is by backwinding. I don't care how experienced an angler you are, but if you play a big, powerful fish by backwinding, you will always give line long before a properly set clutch would yield. By keeping heavy pressure on the fish, it will be landed long before it's totally exhausted.

<u>Pristine tench, like this 8 pounder, demand care and respect</u>

Targeting Extra Big Tench

The first obvious comment to make is that you must select your waters carefully to ensure that they hold the size of fish you seek. In my case, for example, I have access to a cracking tench water that I know can be relied on for a dozen fish on a good day to perhaps over 8lbs. However, the biggest I've ever caught there is 8-6 and I do not know of any 9lb plus fish being reported. So, the fishing is great fun, but if I want to catch more doubles, it is not the water I should be on. By and large, and as a real generalisation, large, lightly stocked gravel pits are where the chances of real monsters are highest, but where you'll wait longest between bites. I am thinking here of the Lea Valley pits, where my old mate Phil Smith has recently landed an enormous fish of 12lb 1oz.

One of the best big tench waters in the country, Bawburgh near Norwich

If you are not interested though in chasing around the country for the ultimate waters, but just want to catch the biggest tench possible from the more normal venues, there are only two methods I know of that have definitely produced bigger than average fish for the water concerned.
The first method I know for certain that has produced the biggest fish in a syndicate water is long term baiting with HP milk protein boilies of a large size, exactly as I've often described for barbel. In my chub book I mentioned the phenomenon that we had discovered, in that the chub on the Ouse that we took on milk protein baits were of a significantly greater average size than the norm. Whether that was down to a factor of bait size or bait type is not clear. A good friend Keith, who has done far more of this specialised boilie fishing for tench than I have, insists that it is a combination of both factors. There is no doubt whatever that HP milk protein baits are highly attractive to fish of all species and by combining this fact with a bait size that only the biggest tench can get in its mouth should automatically ensure that all your tench are big ones. I know that sounds comically simplistic but Keith's catches provide impressive evidence. No angler I know has taken so many doubles in such a short time.

HNV paste wrapped milk protein boilie

The drawback to the regular HP prebaiting approach is that it needs to be carried out regularly to wean the fish on to the bait and it is mighty expensive to do properly. Unless you live close to your water and have very deep pockets, therefore, this is a method requiring total commitment. I am not ashamed to admit that, at my age, I am no longer prepared to go to all the trouble and expense that the method requires to reap the rewards sought.

The method I now use all the time I have christened my hot spot approach, which has been mentioned earlier. Without indulging in undue repetition, I found several years ago that mass baiting with live maggots attracted masses of smaller tench into the swim, particularly males. I could imagine these smaller tench dashing all over the place looking for the escaping grubs, much as small chub chase bits of bread mash downstream. When I first began baiting with dead maggots in the loose feed and confined live grubs to the feeders only, and also enclosed the feeders in a method ball, I immediately noticed a significant increase in the size of tench caught. This was mainly because the number of females in catches was far higher. Quite obviously, this is by no means a foolproof approach to catching the biggest fish in a water, but my results have certainly shown that it works. It has been a long time since I caught really small tench. To give a recent example, a pit I was fishing has a large head of males in the 3lb to 5lb class as well as some big females to over 10lbs. In a catch of 13 tench, I only had one male of around 4lb. The rest were females, with only one fish under 7lbs and three over 8lbs. Those results are far too lop sided to be coincidental, in my opinion. Give it a go and see what you think.

Gorgeous fish of exactly 10lbs

Big Tench Tales

A specimen size for fish is hard to define, but in my formative years of specimen hunting it always seemed easier than it is today. Certainly, from the late fifties until the mid seventies or thereabouts, the accepted level for a "specimen "of all species remained relatively static. In the case of tench, the goal posts determining specimen status have shifted quite dramatically since then. From a huge tench being a fish over 6lbs in 1970, it had to be over 8lbs by 1980. I had my first fish over this weight in 1984, with a brace of 8-4 and 8-14 from Dean's Farm, but they were still rare enough for 8lb to be the target to aim for. By the nineties, however, eight pounders were becoming commonplace and the benchmark for a specimen fish had moved to 9lbs. As far as I am concerned, this is still the target weight when I start to view tench as exceptional specimens, with the magical double figure fish the holy grail of tench angling.

In this section, therefore, I will tell you about tench captures from still waters where I achieved and exceeded the 9lb target. The only exception is on the river Ouse. A river tench of 8lbs plus is still a very rare beast and is my target in this branch of my specimen hunting.

Oxford Pit

In April 2006, an Oxfordshire gravel pit that two friends were fishing produced a mammoth tench of 12lb 7ozs as well as several other doubles. I had been contemplating joining the club and that news made my mind up, in spades! When I arrived at the pit for my first session, I eventually selected a swim on the east bank and found a pronounced drop off from the shallow margins only 25 yards from the bank. I have always preferred close range fishing for tench and I felt sure that tench would patrol that drop off when they commenced earnest spring feeding. Also, the east bank would first feel any warming effect of milder air being carried in by the moderate south westerly wind. After a really cold winter and early spring, which had seen constant biting easterlies, I felt this would be a distinct advantage.

As I felt that the odd fish was all I could realistically hope for, as the water would still be quite cold, I needed to err on the side of caution as far as loose feeding was concerned. So I introduced just a pint each of casters, hemp and small pellets on two areas a few yards apart along the drop off. The hook bait would be red maggots fished in conjunction with Kamasan black cap feeders. The only maggots introduced to the swim would be via the feeders, so that the hook baits would be natural "hot spots".

As the morning wore on, the wind progressively strengthened to a biting north westerly and I was soon dressed more for winter piking than spring tenching. My confidence was waning in the very unappetising conditions, but, at exactly midday, the bobbin on the right hand rod shot to the butt, the alarm screamed, and the reel began backwinding furiously. From the way this first fish was fighting, it was obviously a big male. On the scales, the fish went 6lb 2ozs, one of the biggest male tench I'd ever taken. It was a cracking start and a great confidence booster.

9lb 2ozs from the Oxford pit

My second bite came at 2.30pm, another violent take on the right hand rod. It soon became obvious that I was again connected to a big male tench and a few minutes later I was admiring a new personal best male of 7lb 3ozs. What a clonking fish that was. It was encouraging to see the caster shells in the landing net; the fish were obviously feeding well, which was confirmed within seconds of the rod being recast. I was just setting the bobbin when the line was whipped out of my fingers and the reel spool began spinning furiously. Soon, another chunky male joined the party, a smaller fish of 5lb 14ozs. This was turning out to be quite a session.

The next indications came just after 4pm, on one of those rare occasions when two bites occur exactly simultaneously. Totally synchronised, the bobbins on both rods rose together and both reels began backwinding rapidly. Both fish were safely landed somehow. I played the first tench into the net before even striking the second run, and then was amazed to find the second fish still attached. The result was another superb brace of male tench, of 5lb 10ozs and 6lb 6ozs. It was becoming obvious that the rough conditions had turned the fish on to the feed in quite dramatic fashion. That being the assumption, I topped up the feed with a further helping of the mixed particles.

Although I was completely delighted with the action so far, I was desperate for one of the big females to put in an appearance, but I would have to wait a while longer. As darkness closed in, two more males of exactly 6lbs and 6lb 15oz came in quick succession. As darkness fell, I was expecting the action from tench to cease, as I have never rated night fishing for tench. That night, though, three more fish came in the hours 2.00am to 4.00am, still to the same tactics. These comprised two more clonking males of 6lb 9ozs and 5lb 14oz, plus the only female tench I was to catch, and bizarrely the smallest of the tench I landed at 5lb 6ozs.

I fully expected the dawn period to be hectic, as I rate it the best time for tench on all waters, and yet with the coming of daybreak, the action ceased altogether. At 8.00am, with another six hours to fish before I had to make tracks for home, I introduced the last of my casters, about a pint. As the hours ticked by, the wind became a real problem, continually lifting the rods off the rests. At 11.00am, still biteless, I had just about decided to give it best when, suddenly, a rod was shaking in the rests, the alarm was shrieking and I was in action once more. Soon, another male tench of 5lb 9oz was in the net, to be quickly followed by another of 5lb 13ozs. At 1.00pm, with no further fish, I'd had enough. Buffeted by the gale, soaked by spray, it was more like cod fishing the North Sea than tench fishing at a gravel pit.

On that first spring tench session I landed a total of twelve tench, with a female of 5lb 6ozs and eleven males of between 5lb 9oz and 7lb 3ozs. Remarkably, as well as the seven pounder, there were a further five over six pounds, quite a stunning average. As well as the tench, I took five rudd from 1lb 8oz to 2lb 5oz, and roach of 1lb 11ozs and 1lb 12ozs.

Second nine pounder in two days, 9lb 9ozs

On my second session, I thought that I must improve the ratio of females to males. I couldn't be as unlucky as 1:11 again surely. In fact, that second session saw that trend totally reversed. In the same swim again, using the same tactics, I took a total of 14 tench, and this time it was twelve to two in favour of females. The two males were both five pounders but all twelve females were 6lbs plus, with five over seven pounds. But it was the last two fish of each afternoon that made my spring tenching. On the first day, the swim had gone quiet after a flurry of action around midday and as it approached 4.00pm I was thinking that the next chances I would get would possibly be around dusk but more likely at dawn the next morning. Then, after almost four uneventful hours, the right hand alarm was screaming and I found myself attached to something a good deal more powerful than anything I had yet connected with. The fish fought incredibly hard but eventually I was able to slide it into the net. It was a big female, not at all spawny, and thumped the Avons down to 9lb 2ozs.

On day two, there was a repeat performance. Again, the morning was all go with several tench and rudd brought to net, and again bites ceased quite suddenly at about 1.0pm. This time, it was close to 5.00pm when I was suddenly shocked out of my drowsiness by an intense shrieking from the alarm. This time, the fish did appear to be carrying a modest amount of spawn and, once again, I had a nine pounder. 9lb 9ozs this second leviathan went and still remains the biggest I have ever caught there.

Horseshoe

One of the most famous carp waters in the country is Horseshoe Lake near Lechlade. As well as the carp, though, the water contains impressively sized coarse fish of other species too, notably bream, rudd, pike and especially tench. Several doubles have been taken there. When I made my first trip to Horseshoe in the spring of 2009 I had big tench in mind, with the famous Summer Bay my first destination. Having cast around with a marker float, I was quite surprised how shallow the bay was but pleased that the bottom weed situation looked easily manageable. When I started my normal baiting routine, using lots of mixed particles, the only thing giving me slight concern was the numbers of tufties. However, as I would be fishing at short range, I didn't feel the tuftie menace would be too troublesome. What I didn't know at the time was that there were squadrons of swans about to invade from winter bay, and I'd baited within swan neck range. Within half an hour, I was plagued with dozens of those obnoxious creatures, which made serious angling a test of patience, to say the least. In the two days at my disposal, I had but two tench, which came simultaneously in mid afternoon on the second day. They were both lovely spawned out females of around 6lbs and they at least saved a blank.

Beautiful Horseshoe lake

On my second trip the following week, I decided to try the deeper Winter Bay, where the bait would be out of reach of the swans. I had decided on a heavy baiting approach and introduced several kilos of mixed particles over two spots at forty yards. Plumbing had revealed a bottom of fine silkweed with some pondweed forming, so I elected to fish two red maggots popped up about an inch on a size 12. The second rod was baited with two buoyant rubber red maggots, hair rigged so that the bait hovered over the weed to the length of the hair. At the time, I had never before used rubber baits on their own, lacking the confidence to do so. I'd always had to include at least one real one. But, having spoken to Terry Lampard when he'd outlined the numbers of fish he'd caught just on rubber, I decided to give it a go. It certainly made the required presentation simple to attain.

__8lb 5ozs of Horseshoe tench__

I had the required confidence booster shortly after when an 8lb 5oz fish roared off with the bait. Just on dusk I had another fish four ounces smaller and then it went quiet for the dark hours. The next day it really kicked off, with the first of thirteen tench streaking away with the maggots at first light. Fish came steadily until I packed up in late afternoon, by which time I'd taken a cracking catch of tench, with fish up to 8lb 6ozs.
I was back in the same swim the following week, and this time I fished in incessant rain for the duration of the session. With the rain full in my face it was far from pleasant, but the fishing made up for it. Although not as many fish came to net as the previous week, the average size was better. In all, I caught just seven tench, all over 7lbs, including the one and only nine pounder I've taken from Horseshoe to date. That fish, of 9lb 2oz, was caught just after the heavens had opened with a thunderous downpour.
Since that day, I have never done as well with tench as during that first season, and I know that others fared similarly. The tenching became quite tough, with occasional red letter days to somebody followed by nothing being caught for a week or two. Nevertheless, in between the blanks, I did have some nice tench to 8lb 11ozs, plus a bonus 16lb common carp on rubber casters one night. Horseshoe is still a very challenging water, but it's a gorgeous fishery, very well run, and it contains some stunning fish. Even better, you no longer need to

be a Carp Society member to fish the place. It is available on a £10 per day permit at the time of writing.

<u>My biggest Horseshoe tench, 9lb 2ozs</u>

Syndicate Water
My personal best tench of 8lb 14ozs in 1984 from Deans Farm remained my biggest for another nine years, although I did equal it at a new syndicate water in 1991. The summer of 1993 proved to be a great tench period, and started brilliantly when the very first session on June 16th/17th produced eleven tench up to 8lb 11ozs, a catch that also included two other eight pounders. Those fish came on feeder tactics and the only negative on that trip was losing a colossal tench when the hooklink snapped. I saw the fish a few yards out before the sickening loss and it was certainly well over nine pounds.

For my second session the following week, I again used simple free running open ended feeders, fished above a twelve inch hooklink to a size 14 Drennan Carbon Specimen hook. Bait was two flavoured white maggots, in conjunction with groundbait plugs consisting of breadcrumbs laced liberally with molasses. In the half light of a very misty dawn, the first job was to bombard the swim with a gallon of maggots and a gallon of hemp, sealed in a baiting cone with molasses laced fine breadcrumbs. It was 6.00am before I was relaxing with the first cup of tea of the day, sitting behind two rods. After three uneventful hours a bobbin suddenly hurtled to the butt and I struck into a satisfyingly heavy resistance. The speed of the fish told me that I was attached to a good male and after a few minutes a muscular fish eventually rolled into the net, registering 6lb 2ozs on my Avons. After that first tench, bites came steadily and as dusk approached a further fifteen fish had been netted. The biggest of these weighed 7lb 2ozs, 7lb 4ozs, 7lb 6ozs, 7lb 10ozs and 8lb 3ozs, and it was a memorable session.

The next morning, after another big male of 6lb 14ozs at first light, I then had the dilemma of two big fish on at once. As a good tench surged through a weedbed to my right, the other alarm shrieked out and that rod shook in the rests as another tench rocketed away. Seconds later, I stood in the margins with two rods well bent, as big tench headed off in opposite directions. As the first tench to be hooked felt by far the heavier, I placed the left hand rod back on the rests with the pick up open and continued to play the other fish. Several more minutes elapsed before I netted a fat female that looked a good seven pounder. Leaving the fish in the landing net I picked up the second rod and found that the fish was still attached. The fight it gave was quite tame in comparison but when I eventually landed it I was amazed to find it was far bigger than the first. In order of appearance, those fish went 7lb 13ozs and 8lb 7ozs, a quite stunning brace. After that breathtaking few minutes, I had to endure many biteless hours in the blistering hot sun.

In fact, it was early evening before there were any further signs of tench activity. I remember reaching out for a recast when, suddenly, the reel handle was a blur as another heavy fish powered off. A dogged battle then followed in the deep channel beyond the marginal weed fringe. Slowly I began to gain the ascendancy, as the fish's surges became shorter, but then the tench suddenly shot towards me, burying itself solidly in the vegetation. After several minutes of stalemate, I slowly increased pressure and then the rod tip gradually eased back. All of a sudden, there was a frantic pull, an impressive boil under the surface, and then the tench rocketed back out into deep water. A large raft of pond weed floated to the surface where the fish had been and I gave a silent prayer of thanks that it had broken away as it had. I was never again in serious trouble with the fish, although it was a further good few minutes before I was able to net it. As soon as it lay in the mesh, I could see that the tench was indeed as memorable as had been the scrap it had given me. It weighed 9lb 10ozs, easily a new best and was followed in the next two hours by three other fabulous tench of 7lb 6oz, 7lb 14ozs and 8lb 13ozs, to draw the curtain down on a truly unforgettable trip.

Returning my 9lb 10oz fish

The five years that followed that exciting summer were barren tench wise, with very few fish taken. A large shallow acreage is totally inaccessible and it is probable that under certain weather and water conditions the tench may stay in that area, immune from the attentions of anglers. However, my very first session of 1998 was to coincide with witnessing the first double figure tench I'd ever seen, in the shape of a truly awesome fish of 10lb 10ozs. As you might imagine, I was now really buzzing but by July, I'd only managed two big fish amongst twenty much smaller specimens. The two big ones weighed 8lb 13ozs and 9lb 2ozs, so I was happy with a second "nine". I was approaching my tench fishing in the usual manner, with lots of bait, but noticed that other anglers were using no bait at all other than what was in their feeders. Over the first few weeks, three of these anglers took just one fish apiece in a day session, but all three fish were ten pounders. I felt that three huge fish caught in the same manner could not be coincidence.

It was becoming evident that my comparatively heavy baiting was attracting plenty of fish but obviously reducing my chances of a really big one. With that in mind, I decided on a complete change. Instead of gallons of hemp, maggots, casters and particles, I used just three small spods of hemp, mixed with two pints of casters and a few mini halibut pellets. Also, rather than an accurate heavy concentration of feed, which I'd always favoured, I made sure the three spods were well scattered. Hopefully the big fish would see nothing alarming in this presentation. I also eliminated pints of live maggots in the free feed, which had probably led to the large number of average fish I'd had in my swims on the sessions so far. From now on, I'd only use maggots in my feeders, to give a focal point.

My first session to the new approach is one of the highlights of my angling life. In fact, I consider the catch of tench that followed the greatest catch of specimen fish of my entire career. The first day was quiet, and the only action I had was a 2lb perch to my maggots. The next morning dawned warm, sultry and overcast, with frequent light showers, and I was soon to hook and lose a real monster of a tench in a dense weedbed. I never had time to curse that loss too long as, at 6.30am, the bobbin again rose slowly to the butt ring. As I set the hook, a powerful fish surged to my right, where there was a pronounced headland and weedbed which had proved my earlier undoing. With this second fish, however, it was turned from danger in the nick of time and there were then no further dramas. A few minutes later a monstrous tench rolled into the waiting net. As soon as I peeled the mesh back I knew what I had and when the Avons confirmed 10lb 3ozs it was a moment of pure elation. If I hadn't had another bite that day it wouldn't have mattered, but in fact the action was only just beginning.

Less than a minute after recasting, the reel handle was again spinning crazily as another big tench sprinted off to my right. Five minutes later I was confirming 9lb 12ozs. What an amazing few minutes; I'd just taken my two biggest tench ever in successive casts. I just couldn't take it in but if I'd been told what was about to transpire I wouldn't have believed it. I had just recast once more and was in the process of taking in the slack when the rod lurched forward. Yet another big fish shot off with the bait; it must have taken the maggots on the drop. As I bent into the fish, such was its power and weight that I doubted it could possibly be a tench. The longer the battle went on the more convinced I became that I had foul hooked one of the very big pike the water contained. I thought I must have cast across its back, causing it to bolt and hook itself. There was absolutely no stopping it; the fish had already surged way past the little headland to my right, a good forty yards away, so that the line was now parallel to the bank and actually running through the branches of a bankside alder. The only choice I had was to clamp down hard or lose the fish anyway. I held on grimly, my hand clamped over the reel, and the line reached that tinny stage when you can hear the high pitched whistle in the wind. Any moment now, I thought, the line's going to give or the pike will bite through the hooklink. But everything held and then, miraculously, the rod eased back as the fish began to yield. There then followed a heart stopping ten minutes as line was retrieved jerkily through a tangle of branches. When it was within about twenty yards, the fish suddenly decided on a determined dash offshore which, amazingly, saw the line ping free of the tree. Ten yards out, it rolled for the first time. Instead of the pike I was expecting, there in front of me was one awesome giant of a tench. I think I stopped breathing as the fish covered those last few yards into the waiting net, and then the euphoria took over. A few moments later, anglers from nearby swims were on hand to confirm the fish at 11lb 11oz; never in my wildest dreams did I ever expect to catch such a monstrous tench. In less than an hour, I'd banked three tench for an aggregate of 31lb 10oz.

With those three magnificent fish returned, and me relaxing in my bivvy with a fresh cup of tea as heavy rain pounded down, I relived those incredible few minutes over and over again. In

Tench of 9-12, 10-3 and 11-11

fact, there were no further bites until early afternoon, when I had two more fish in quick succession. These tench took the scales to 9lb 4oz and 9lb 2oz. What an astonishing average, which became even more astonishing in early evening when my sixth and last tench of the day weighed in at exactly 10lbs. When I calculated that the six fish had totalled exactly

60lbs, giving an average of dead on 10lbs, there was something magical about those statistics. The actual session was far from over, though, as in just three hours on the final morning, before I left for home, I managed a further four fish, two at 8lb 14ozs, plus fish of 9lb 3ozs and 9lb 6ozs. In total, the session had yielded ten tench for an aggregate weight of 96lbs 5ozs, the most awesome tench fishing I've ever experienced or ever likely to experience.

My personal best tench of 11lb 11ozs

Upper Great Ouse

As I said earlier in this book, tench fishing on the Great Ouse is a comparatively recent activity, as it was only a few years ago that I realised the species existed in sufficient numbers to make their pursuit worthwhile. From 2005, I had a few sessions each summer and by June 2011 I'd had a lot of fish, with the best 7lb 11oz. By still water standards, that is a modest fish but is exceptional for a river tench.

I've had some very interesting river tenching since the 2011 summer, in the company of my good friend Alan Lawrence. We have both had lots of fish to over 7lbs and the most memorable session was in late July when we were both plagued by signal crayfish. On the first night of a two night trip, we had both been using 14mm boilies with few problems, taking good bream and tench regularly. On the second night, the crays had found our baits and using boilies became virtually impossible. At dusk, though, before he had been forced to switch to rubber corn, Alan landed a lovely tench of 6lb 14ozs that had tail damage undoubtedly caused by an otter attack. I was fishing about thirty yards upstream of Alan and about an hour after dawn I had a good run on two grains of popped up rubber corn and duly landed the same tench, still weighing 6lb 14ozs. At the time, we christened it the Friendly Tench.

Fourth capture of the Friendly tench in three seasons, 7lb 6ozs

Fast forward now to August 2012 and we're back on the stretch but well over a quarter of a mile upstream. Once again, plenty of tench and bream came our way and on the second day, just before dark, Alan shouted that he'd caught Old Friendly again. I went down for a look and, sure enough, it was undoubtedly the same fish. Over the year, it had gained three ounces and now took the scales to 7lb 1oz. If I now take you to just a few weeks ago, early July 2013, Alan and I settled into the swims we had fished in 2011. We both wondered whether we would see Old Friendly for a fourth time! I started off on the first night presenting my old favourite 14mm Crustacean Cocktail boilies. These were fished on a size 8 Pallatrax hook to six inches of green braid, using an in line Stonze as a method feed holder. The method ball consisted of Bloodworm method mix, into which a generous amount of hemp, corn and stewed wheat had been mixed, as well as a good glug of liquid molasses. As well as the method, the swim was primed with a dozen Spombs of mixed hemp, corn and wheat plus an initial helping of 60 boilies.

Alan was fishing similarly with his own version of what I was doing, and it was fairly quiet for both of us until darkness began to close in, although we had made our first casts in mid afternoon. That first night, though, was manic. Between us we had 14 bream to almost nine pounds, evenly split between us, plus a couple of 5lb tench. With no sleep whatever, we both grabbed a few hours during the heat of the second day and began serious fishing again on the second afternoon. The action started again almost immediately after I had introduced more feed, but I was soon forced to switch my hook bait to two grains of popped up rubber corn. The infamous Ouse crayfish had found the bed of bait and boilies were being destroyed in double quick time.

There was no let up in the action though, and from early evening until dark good bream and tench came regularly, plus a hard fighting 12lb common to Alan. As soon as darkness fell, however, the second night was in total contrast to the first. Alarms fell silent and remained that way until just after 3.00am. Then there was a sudden scream from my right hand alarm. I must have jumped a foot but still managed to do everything correctly and found myself attached to a very muscular adversary. All tench fight, but river tench seem to have that little extra zip, and it was a good few minutes before I managed to slip the net under it. As I turned on the head torch to examine my prize, there in the mesh reposed the unmistakeable Friendly Tench. Soon I confirmed 7-6 and shouted Alan. He couldn't believe it either, nor that I'd caught the fish in total darkness. In all my years tenching on all waters, I've caught very few in the dark and I'd never had a night caught river tench. So, all in all, it was a memorable capture. When we packed up on Friday morning, between us we'd taken 32 bream, with a top fish each of 8-14, plus nine tench and the one carp. My 7-6 was the biggest tench but there had been three others over 6lbs.

On the very first trip of the 2012 campaign, in July, I was to take my personal best river tench to over 8lbs. After early season floods, mid July at last found the river at normal height and clarity. Once again, I was fishing with Alan, in swims about forty yards apart. I fished the first night on my own, Alan joining me the next morning. The stretch is wider than average for the upper Ouse, fairly clear of bottom weed but featuring wide lily bed margins along both banks. The tench particularly colonise these lilies and we've found that by targeting any little bays in the cabbages we can create small hot spots. For the carp, they tend to hold off the lilies toward the deeper water and the usual approach is to put one bait hard against the cabbages under the opposite bank, but drop the other bait a few yards short.

I started to prepare my swim at around midday, baiting with around 100 15mm boilies initially, plus several Spombs full of hemp and corn. I would be fishing method feeders, with a method ball packed with corn around my Stonze weight on each cast. The reason for the heavy corn contribution was because of the signal crayfish problem. As I said earlier, in 2011, after the first day catching on boilies, the crays moved in and made boilie fishing impossible. A switch to rubber corn caught a couple of tench. This year, at the slightest sign of signal interference, I would revert to popped up rubber corn on both rods.

I made my first casts at around 4.00pm. I was unprepared for quite such an instant reaction because, only twenty minutes later, I'd already caught two tench, both just over six pounds. They gave lightening fast runs, just like carp. River tench really are an exciting quarry. The third tench was the fish I'd set my heart on. After a great battle in and out of the far bank lilies I finally had the upper hand and slid the net under a very big tench. When I confirmed 8lb 2oz I was over the moon. The rest of the evening continued in similar vein, with four more tench falling to my boilies and no apparent interference from signals. As darkness fell, however, I started to get little twitches and gently wound in to find boilies nibbled away and hair stops miraculously removed. It was time for the rubber corn and thereafter the signal problem stopped. I had one more tench before it became completely dark, a lovely 7-4 specimen, and then the bream moved in. I had five of them in the dark hours, to a little over 7lbs, but there was no sign of a carp run.

Best tench yet from the Great Ouse 8lb 2ozs

Alan joined me in late morning and was as delighted as I'd been with my 8lb tench. He prepared his swim exactly as I'd prepared mine, with the exception that he started on the rubber corn from the off. In my swim, I reverted to boilies when I restarted fishing, and did catch one nice tench and two bream before the crays moved in again. By tea time I was on rubber corn on both rods, which produced three more tench before dark. Strangely, the second night was completely blank; I never had a twitch in the dark hours. Only as dawn was breaking did I get another couple of fish before it was time to go.

I've had to adjust my river tench sights to 9lb now; never satisfied, are we!

This would be some river tench! 10lb 3ozs

Conclusion

To a tench angler, is there any more emotive sight, in the mist of a calm summer dawn, than the huge patch of frothy bubbles that have suddenly appeared around the float? All round, lily pads shake as more tench head for the banquet he has laid. As the float trembles, his hand hovers over the rod butt in barely controlled anticipation. Then, it tilts and slides away, disappearing under the oily smooth water. The battle is joined and soon a beautiful, glossy green creature reposes in the landing net.

This scenario, to me, is the true essence of tench fishing, the real magic. I enjoy the windswept pits, searching for leviathans, as I do the huge daunting reservoirs, and I will always spend the bulk of my big tench fishing time on those waters. However, nothing comes close to the aesthetic pleasure of the tench fishing to be had on small, lily strewn estate lakes. Each summer, I make a point of early morning sessions on such waters, fishing a simple lift float at the side of the lily pads. The first tench I ever caught, well over fifty years ago, was taken this way and I have loved the method ever since.

What a brace, 8lb 13ozs and 9lb 2ozs

Tony Miles

November 2014

Printed in Great Britain
by Amazon